THE SERMONS OF REV. W.B. SEALS

A Preacher/Teacher in Service to the Lord

Compiled and Edited by
Barbara A. Seals Nevergold, PhD

Copyright © 2013 by Barbara A. Seals Nevergold, PhD. 128575-NEVE
ISBN: Softcover   978-1-4797-8337-3
        EBook   978-1-4797-8338-0

All rights reserved. No part of this book may be reproduced or transmitted in any form or by any means, electronic or mechanical, including photocopying, recording, or by any information storage and retrieval system, without permission in writing from the copyright owner.

To order additional copies of this book, contact:
Xlibris Corporation
1-888-795-4274
www.Xlibris.com
Orders@Xlibris.com

The Sermons of Rev. W.B. Seals

    This photo of Rev. Seals was taken in 1958 or 1959. He is dressed to attend a function, probably an anniversary dinner, at Cold Spring Baptist Church or St. John Baptist Church. Also, he may have taken his own photo as he often set up his camera with a timer to snap self-portraits.

The Sermons of Rev. W.B. Seals

THE ORIGINS OF THIS BOOK

My father was a man of many talents. In addition to being a man of the gospel, he was a talented musician and an expert photographer. His photography career spanned nearly a half-century and produced thousands of photographs and negatives. Following his death in 1995, members of the family decided to gather as many images as possible, especially the early ones. However, the search that the family conducted for the negatives and photos that chronicle our father's photographic career resulted in finding materials that are equally emblematic of his role as a minister of the Gospel.

We found an unexpected treasure in the copies of the notes that he used to construct his sermons. These hand-written notes were probably also used when he preached. Many were dated and cited the church where they were delivered. The earliest one dated to 1948 with the last ones ending in 1988. Surprisingly many of the messages he conveyed have a timeless nature to them as the issues which he addressed are still relevant! This small volume is also enriched by copies of photos taken from our father's collection and scans of some of the original notes.

The majority of the sermons in this book were preached during Dad's pastorate of the Cold Spring Baptist Church in Buffalo, New York. He was the pastor of Cold Springs, located at Verplanck and Woodlawn Avenues, from about 1956 to 1961. During the latter part of his tenure at the Church his sermons show signs of mounting frustration and difficulties with a faction of the congregation. I leave the analysis of this period of my father's ministry to the reader, but I think that these sermons provide an interesting picture of the management problems that many ministers encounter in their positions as spiritual as well as organizational leaders.

Finally, we were extremely fortunate that these papers weren't over-looked and destroyed. I have to give special acknowledgement to my brothers, James, John and Jerry for their foresight in gathering these sermons, the negatives and photographs for preservation. Initially, I transcribed these sermons/notes and saved them to be shared with the family. It's taken over 15 years but finally they can be passed down to a generation, who were not even alive when our father died.

However, I believe that these papers represent not just a family legacy as they illustrate a tradition of the Black ministry. Like so many of his peers, our father was an itinerant minister, who answered his call to ministry while keeping his day job (in my father's case, day jobs). This little book offers a glimpse into the life of a Black man, born more than a century ago, who persevered against the challenges of his day to succeed in several chosen fields.

Rev. W. B. Seals' Children
Left to right:
Back row: David, Bruce, Kenneth, Jerry, James and Frank
Front Row: Mildred, Barbara, John and Willie

Dad's parents were Joseph (Giuseppe) Nasello and Irene Lair. Joseph Nasello, a native of Gangi, a town in Sicily, was born May 5, 1875. He immigrated to Louisiana in 1901. He was a dry goods merchant, who operated a store in downtown Alexandria. He died on April 2, 1959.

Irene Lair was born on August 15, 1894 in Bayou Rapides, near Alexandria, LA. She died in Buffalo, NY on September 27, 1946. She is buried in the family church's cemetery in Bayou Rapides.

This photo of Dad and his sister, Alice (Seals Jones Lewis) was taken in 1922. Note the black drape placed on the side of the house where the photograph was taken. This is the only known photograph of the Seals children. Dad was about 12 at the time of this picture and Aunt Alice was about 10 years old.

BIOGRAPHICAL SKETCH: REVEREND WILLIE BROWN SEALS
NOVEMBER 22, 1910 – APRIL 19, 1995

Willie Brown Seals, who preferred to be known by his initials, W.B., was born on November 22, 1910 in the rural community of Bayou Rapides, near Alexandria, Louisiana. He was the eldest child and only son of Irene Lair. His only sibling, Alice Roosevelt Seals, was born two years later. Their father, Giuseppe Nasello was a native of Sicily, who immigrated to this country in 1901.

Giuseppe, or Joe, was married during the time of his relationship with Irene Lair, and never acknowledged his son or daughter. He owned a dry goods store in Alexandria. Although W.B. would tell the story of how his mother would take him to his father's store where she was given items for her children; it's unlikely that father and son ever met formally. Nasello died in 1959 leaving seven other children, three daughters and four sons.

The origin of the Seals name has some mystery attached to it, as neither child was given their mother's surname of Lair. According to W.B. "Seals" was a name, he made up. He claimed to have taken the name, from a favorite teacher, named Lucille Seal. Initially, he omitted the "s" from the spelling. He said he added it later, because Seals sounded better than Seal. The 1920 census confirms that the name was originally spelled "Seal", but Willie was uncertain as to when the alteration was made. There were Seals families in the Alexandria region, but no information has been found to confirm any relationship with these families.

W.B. and his sister Alice grew up in the cities of Alexandria and Lake Charles, Louisiana. He attended schools in both cities; however his formal education ended after the sixth grade. In later years, he enjoyed telling the story of how he perfected his reading ability by reading the newspapers used to "wall paper" his family's shanty home. At an early age, he demonstrated musical ability and was allowed to take piano lessons with a local teacher. The piano student quickly became an adept musician who mastered classical pieces as well as traditional gospel and spirituals. In his early twenties, he became the choral director, pianist and organist for several churches in the Alexandria area. He also earned extra money by giving music lessons to adult as well as children piano students.

At age 23, W.B. answered a calling to the ministry. His formal ordination did not take place until 1954, yet the ministry marked a life-long avocation that lead the Rev. W.B. Seals to pastor several churches in the Alexandria area, and later in Buffalo and Niagara Falls, New York. At one point, he experienced a personal conflict between his musical calling and his spiritual calling. However, he decided to pursue the ministry as he felt he "had a greater conviction for the ministry." He continued, however, to teach piano and to play for groups in his church, when requested.

In fact, after his move to Buffalo, he responded to the request of young people at the St. John Baptist Church, to assist them in starting a choir. The Bells of St. John organized under Rev. Seals' leadership, in 1948, continued to provide musical accompaniment to the church service for over a half century. He also mentored other young musicians. Carole Varner, St. John's Minister of Music in the 1970s acknowledged his mentoring influence on her musical development.

In 1931, Rev. Seals married Nettie Mae Patterson. They had four children, Willie Patterson, John Douglas, Mildred Irene and James Charles. A decade later, the couple divorced and in what was an unusual ruling at the time; Rev. Seals was given custody of their four children. A second marriage took place in 1943. And a year later, Willie and the former Clara Ellis added a fifth child, Barbara Ann, to their family. By 1944, the Seals family had settled into routine life in Alexandria. In addition to teaching piano in his home, acting as choral director and pianist for several churches and pastoring his own church, Rev. Seals also maintained a full-time job at an auto-parts store.

In 1943, Irene Lair, Rev. Seals' mother suffered an incapacitating stroke. Her daughter Alice, who had recently moved to Buffalo, moved Irene to Buffalo to take care of her. Irene Lair's death in September 1946 set into motion a chain of events that resulted in major life changes for the Seals family. At the urging of his sister, Rev. Seals agreed to move to Buffalo so that the two siblings and their families could be together. The following year, the Seals family joined the historic exodus of Black emigrants from the South that has been described as the Second Great Migration. In the decade between 1940 and 1950, the black population of Buffalo swelled from 18,000 to 36,745. Like many of their compatriots, who were sheltered by family until they found jobs and could get established, the seven members of the Seals family moved in with Rev. Seals' sister, her husband John and teen-aged daughter, Dorothy.

The apartment that the family shared at 266 Walnut Street near Broadway was typical of Buffalo's Black neighborhoods at that time; very old and crowded housing stock. The Seals family lived in the lower-front residence in a four apartment building. Their cold—water flat consisted of four rooms: a living room, kitchen, and two small bedrooms. The lavatory comprised of only a commode and basin was located in the hall and shared with the back apartment. Rev. Seals found work at the Chevrolet Plant on River Road in Tonawanda and worked there for almost twenty-five years until his retirement in 1972. The family also grew as four sons; Gerald, Kenneth, Bruce and David were born between 1950 and 1962 following the move to Buffalo.

In spite of the fact that he worked a full time job, Rev. Seals became an active participant in Buffalo's religious community. He was well known as a preacher, teacher and church musician. Soon after their arrival in Buffalo, the Seals family joined the congregation of St. John Baptist Church and became active and involved members. Rev. and Mrs. Seals remained life-long members of St. John's. He served as the Assistant and Associate pastor of the church as well as Bible study and Sunday school teachers. After his retirement, he served as a pastoral minister visiting and ministering to the sick and shut-in members of the congregation.

For extended periods, he also ministered to other congregations outside of the St. John congregation. In 1956, he was called to the pastorate of the Cold Spring Baptist Church and remained there until the early 1960s leading the congregation in retiring its mortgage debt and significantly increasing its membership. In succeeding years, he was interim Pastor of the New Hope Baptist Church in Niagara Falls as well as New Hope Baptist Church of Buffalo. He was invited to numerous churches as a guest preacher and Bible study teacher during his many years in the ministry. He attended numerous conventions and convocations of his denomination and also took religious studies classes to expand his Biblical knowledge. Dad summed up his belief about the role of the minister in a newspaper interview. He is quoted as saying that the dedicated minister " . . . is a good teacher and organizer. He should be committed to his calling and the responsibilities God has placed on him."

After his move to Buffalo, he developed an interest in photography. He started photography as a hobby in 1947. Once his interest was aroused, he spent a great deal of time perfecting his photographic techniques and skills. Although he had a mentor, Cornelius Ryer he was largely self-taught. He learned to take the photos, process and develop the negatives and print the pictures as well. He was particularly skilled in lighting and photo composition. Before color photography was available, he hand painted the black and white pictures with oil paints. He spent countless hours at his desk with a paint palate, tubes of oils, q-tips and cotton swabs and painstakingly detailed eyes, hair, cheeks or jewelry with just the right color. In later years, he added special effects photography, such as double exposure and unique backgrounds, to his repertoire.

For nearly 50 years, he built a sideline "job" into a professional business that he named, Seals Ebony Studio. He was called on by myriad groups and individuals to document the history of several generations of African Americans in the Western New York area, from births to deaths, to marriages and other celebrations, to changes in the life of a community over time. After his death in 1995, thousands of carefully preserved, documented (names, dates, addresses) negatives and photographs were found in his filing cabinets. They represent a half-century of photographic records. These negatives and the resultant photographs are extraordinary in that they comprise an intact collection that portrays the rich history of an African American community as seen through the lens of an African American photographic artist.

During his lifetime, he received numerous recognitions from the churches and church groups he worked with. But he was most proud of the citations and proclamations he received from the New York State Governor, Buffalo Mayor and Common Council on the occasion of his 80th birthday in 1990.

In many respects, the story of Willie Brown Seals' life is reflective of the lives of many unheralded African American men, who were born in his era. In spite of the oppression and overt institutional racism that was condoned by the Jim Crow laws and associated societal conventions of the early twentieth century, Willie Brown Seals and many of his contemporaries strived to live lives that were productive, contributory and exemplary in their contributions to their families and communities.

ST JOHN CHURCH BUILDING

St. John Baptist Church – Sycamore & Spruce Streets (photo by Rev. W.B. Seals, 1952)

Soon after moving to Buffalo, our family found a church home at St. John Baptist Church. The church quickly became the center of our social as well as our spiritual life. Dad was not only able to realize his religious calling at St. John but he also contributed to the religious community through his musical talents. As his photographic expertise developed he became the Church's official photographer, recording church organizations and functions, like the Pastor's anniversary celebrations and member's weddings, birthday parties and family reunions. Even after his term as pastor of the Cold Spring Baptist Church and two extended periods as the interim pastor of New Hope Baptist Church in Niagara Falls, he returned to St. John's. He concluded his ministerial career at St. John's as an associate pastor and the pastor of the visitation ministry.

THE BELLS OF ST. JOHN PROGRAM

According to a history of the choir written in 1992: "The Bells of St. John is the third oldest choir of the church . . . In 1948, Rev. W.B. Seals organized the Bells with a group of about twenty-five people. Rev. Seals, being an accomplished pianist and a great advocate of spiritual and classical music encouraged the group to form a choir . . . .

Rev. Seals then became mentor and musical director of the choir. According to records, Rev. Seals was a very conscientious teacher of spiritual hymns and two of the most memorial selections he taught the choir were, "Dwelling in the Beulah Land" and "Oh, How I Love Jesus". After the group became more stabilized, Rev. Seals relinquished the teaching and directing to Andrew Brown, who directed it for 27 years."

SERMONS OF REVEREND WILLIE BROWN SEALS

(Note: These sermons and sermon notes were typed exactly as they were written; leaving spellings, abbreviations, phrasing as they were found in the handwritten copies)

1.
Passing By on The Other Side.   Luke 10:31.

1. The Occasion of this text resulted from a question asked Jesus by a lawyer.

   Jesus was often asked questions.
   1) When he cleansed the temple.
   2) Healing on the sabbath.
   3) His claim to Divine Sonship.
   4) Thomas wanted to know the way
   5) Phillip about the Father.

2.
6. A certain lawyer stood up to tempt Jesus.

   "Master, what shall I do to inherit eternal life?" Jesus Answered, "what is written in the law?"

   The lawyer, willing to justify himself asked, "And who is my neighbor"

7. Jesus gives the

3.
parable verse 10:30.

8. The Priest: A dignitary of the church. Self-exalted, self-centered. Too high to look low.

9. The Levite proud of his racial heritage drew nigh — looked on but had no mercy.

10. The Samaritan: An

4.
Outcast from Jewish society. Hated and despised. Almost regarded as the leavings of the human race.

But he had compassion and went to the rescue of the fallen man.

1. Now which of the 3?
2. Go and do likewise.

Contagious Religion John 4: 28-29, 39, 41-42

April 3, 1948

First, we offer apologies for the use of the word "contagious". This word automatically carries with it the sense of fear because its single, common use expresses dread. Herein is found the miraculous power of a word. The same word used to describe sorrow, distress, death and distinction can also describe happiness, joy and a beautiful life. Contagious means catching, hence catching religion; Contagious Religion.

Some months ago a song came out about setting the world on fire. It is high time that we as Christians, the Light of the World" and "salt" of the earth, would burn with-in with the zeal of God and set the world on fire with the religion of our Lord and Savior Jesus Christ. If this world is to be saved from the doom that lies just ahead it will be saved by the people who have, own and possess a contagious religion.

Some people consider religion a burden. A heavy yoke upon the neck of its possessor. But it is not so. Religion is a pleasure. Religion never was designed to make our pleasure less. To support this Jesus gave the parable of the last coin in which the woman is overcome with joy when she finds her precious piece of silver.

We should be overcome with joy when our catching religion becomes the instrument making us "Fisher of Men", in the true sense of the word.

Samaria before Jesus came; a racial and religious barrier existed between the people of Samaria and their neighbors the Jews. Hate, flaming the prejudice and strife breeded in the hearts of both races, Samaritans and Jews. So is the heart of every unbeliever before Jesus moves in. A heart of hate for his fellow man, in direct opposition to God's command of love, etc., etc.

Samaria after Jesus came, Reformed! Transformed! From ungodliness to Godliness; righteousness and love. (The reformed man of God add)

The final result of one woman with a Contagious Religion; Paul says, Romans 12: 1-2
"I beseech you therefore brethren, by the mercies of God, that ye present your bodies a living sacrifice etc."

The Indestructible (sic) Christ Revelations 1: 18

August 1953

Christ cannot be destroyed. Neither his word; nor his church. But in every age, his enemies have tried to destroy his influence among men.

As Jesus walked along the shore of beautiful Lake Genesanet he lifted up his eyes and just beyond a small grove of trees he saw 2 men fishing. As he drew near he called to them: "Follow me and I will make you to become fishers of men". Immediately they came to shore and dropped their nets. Their names were: James and John, sons of Zebedee.

John became one of Christ's most loyal and trusted disciples.

John's books: the Gospel that bears his name. 1-2-3 John and the Revelations of Jesus Christ. John would never have written this book were it not for the fact he had a faith that could not be moved. Persecuted and imprisoned, he was given choice of denying Christ, stop preaching the gospel and count God's way unholy, or be banished to the lonely island of Patmos in the Aegean Sea. John preferred to be banished from human society and live forever with God.

John knew that Jesus lives

He had seen him on resurrection morning

John was with the disciples in a room behind bolted doors for fear of the Jews when Jesus suddenly appeared in the room. Thomas was not there.

John helped try persuade Thomas Jesus was alive.

Jesus re-appeared for Thomas' benefit. "Behold, my hands, my side" "Lord, I believe." "Blessed are those who have not seen and believe."

John was with the risen Christ when, after 40 days, he led them to Mount Olivet. There he gave to them the great commission. "Go ye into all the world, and preach the gospel."

On the 50th day, the day of Pentecost, John was one of the 12 disciples assembled in the upper room. Singing and praying and being on one accord each with the other.

The Advent of the Holy Spirit "Rushing might wind" – "Filled all the house" – "Cloven tongues like as of fire sat upon each". Each began to speak with "other tongues" as spirit gave utterance. Jacob's dream of Angels ascending and descending on ladders that reached to heaven. "How dreadful is this place", etc. Peter comes to the defense of disciples. Quotes prophecy of Joel. "In the last days." Acts 2:

John on the isle of Patmos, Rev. 1st chapter

9v – I John –brother—companion in tribulation was in isle called Patmos—for word of God –testimony of Jesus Christ

10v – I was I spirit on Lord's day a great voice, as a trumpet

11v – I am Alpha Omega; what thou seest writ in a book – send to 7 churches

12v – And I turned to see voice. 7 golden candlesticks

13v – In midst of 7 candlesticks one like unto son of man clothed with garment down to feet – golden girdle

14v – His head and his hairs, white-wool-snow eyes like as flame of fire.

15v – Feet –brass-voice many waters

16v – Right hand – 7 stars, mouth sharp two edged sword; countenance, sun shineth in strength

17v — Saw him – fell at feet as dead

18v — "I am alive forever more"

Mystery of 7 stars, 7 golden candle sticks; 3: 14 Unto angel-church-Lordica write

I know they works, neither cold nor hot

So then because – lukewarm

Behold I stand at door

Lives That Were Transformed by a Vision — Acts 26: 19

Cold Springs Baptist Church — Nov. 11, 1956 11 a.m.

In our text we have read to you the testimony of a man who had become a prisoner for Jesus Christ. For two long years this man Paul had suffered as a common criminal in Caesarea.

He stood a rigid examination before Gov. Felix and two years later when Felix was replaced by Festus Paul also was brought before him. Now he again makes his defense before King Agrippa. The Bible tells us "The way of a transgressor is hard". Again the Bible says "Be not deceived God is not mocked: whatsoever a man soweth that shall he also reap."

Paul had at one time been a great enemy of the Church. Destroying churches, sending innocent believers to their deaths to satisfy his ungodly heart. It is a dangerous thing to interfere with a child of God. Jesus said "Woe unto him that offend the least of these my little ones." It would be better that a "Mill stone be hanged around his neck and he be cast in the sea than to offend the least of these, my little ones."

All of Heaven is united and all the power of the God-head is directed against that man that tries to destroy the Church of God. When Paul was a young man he too had an indirect part in the stoning of Stephen the first deacon. Although he was too young by law, to cast a stone in the public execution, but he was equally as guilty by association. Because he held the coats of those who did throw the stones.

You may not be directly guilty of cursing out your neighbor but you are still wrong for encouraging your friend to do so. Lives that were transformed by a vision. "O King Agrippa I was not disobedient unto the Heavenly vision."

There are some wives who call themselves good house keepers. Yet they never re-arrange their furniture; never brighten up the home with new drapes at the windows or a few pictures on the wall. There are some husbands who call themselves good providers yet they never replace a broken glass with another piece of glass not as long as a piece of cardboard is handy.

There are some leaders who call themselves good leaders. Yet he is the only one who seems to prosper under his own leadership. Why? The Bible says "Where there is no vision the people perish." and also "the blind cannot lead the blind." So the question is ; how can you show me thing you cannot see yourself. How can you sell me a good luck cross guaranteed to bring me success and happiness when you are out to sell so you can eat? Marconi 1896-1901; Thomas A Edison Alex Gram Bell

Paul's vision on the road to Damascus was no imagination — it was Real; Had the best effect on countless millions. His life was completely changed.

How Much Do You Weigh? — Dan 5: 25-27
Cold Spring Baptist Church — December 2, 1956 11:00 a.m.

On last Sunday evening our choir had a musical program followed by a weight contest. It was both interesting and amusing. We enjoyed a lovely evening.

Man's scales registered only in pounds the flesh, blood and bones: but God's scales weigh the mind, character and soul of man. God's only interest in the physical part of man is that he does not mis-use or abuse his body which does not belong to him. "Know ye not that your bodies are the members of Christ?"

1. I have here an example of how God weighs a man. Belshazzar the ancient King of Babylon inherited the throne upon the death of Nebachadnezza with absolute power; power of life or death over all his subjects.

His kingdom was great. He was rich with much gold, silver and precious stones. In his mighty army he had thousands of chariots; thousands of horse men and foot soldiers to crush weak nations at his will. Too much success is dangerous for some people. It was dangerous for the prodigal son. Belshazzar became lifted up in pride. I am god. No other god exits but me. My father was god before me. Did not my father cause a golden (statue) of himself be made. Did not all the people of Babylon fall down before the golden image at the sound of the music and worship it?

2. He gave a great banquet called for the sacred vessels of the temple of Solomon. God will not allow to go unpunished the man that profane the sacred things This also applies to God's servants. David said to his servant stay thy hand. He is the Lord's anointed. Belshazzar's fatal mistake; Behold I come quickly and my reward etc. The moving hand Daniel interprets the meaning of the hand.

3. How much do you weigh in love? The greatest thing in the world is love. "God is love" and "God so loved the world." Now God commands us to "Love one another". I am sure that if we would cast out our petty differences, try hard to understand each other more and love each other as Christ has told us to do.

Our lives would be happier, our homes more like a home should be. And our church would regain the full strength of its saving power. 1 Can 13 And though I speak with the tongues of men and angels. How much do you weigh in works? Talk is cheap. But it is work that counts. "Faith without works is dead." James admonishes us to "But be ye doers of the word, and not hearers only, deceiving your own selves." "For if any be a hearer of the

Word, and not a doer." Jesus was a tireless worker. "My Father worked heather to and I work." "I must work."

Examples of Christ — John 13:15
Cold Spring Baptist Church — April 7, 1957 11:00 a.m.

We offer you this text in the hope someone will think on his or her ways and pledge anew more loyalty and more allegiance to our Christ and His Kingdom. We readily own Christ as our Lord and Savior. We sing aloud his praises. We lift to high heavens anthems, spirituals and songs of praise as we sing of his excellent and Divine Glory. " He woke me up this morning. He's so good to me". "God will take care of you." and "The Lord will make a way somehow." And countless other songs ascribing to the goodness of God. But we do so little for Him. We are always too tired. Don't feel well enough or any kind of excuse that sounds good to us to cover up for our poor service. Yet we loudly claim Christ as our Christ.

When the Bible says: Freely ye have received, freely give. This did not refer only to money. But freely give of your time, your talents, your substance, your Christian courtesy and kindness. Jesus had this to say about "hearer's" only and "doers" of the word. If any man hear my sayings and doeth them I will liken him unto a wise man who built his house upon a rock." etc. etc. And everyone that hear these sayings and keeps them not is like a foolish man who built his house upon the sands. etc, etc. (Matt. 7:24) James exhorts us to be "doers" also.

1. Christ's example of forgiveness

Christ placed emphasis on forgiveness as a necessary part of the Christian life. In the Lord's Prayer we are taught to pray "Forgive us our trespasses as we have already forgiven those who trespass against us." We cannot come before God with ought in our hearts against our brother. When Christ was dying on the cross, He stopped dying and looked at those that reviled Him as they paraded before the cross and said; "Father forgive them, etc."

Peter one day asked Christ if my brother sin against me how oft shall I forgive him, till seven (7) times? But Jesus answered seventy times 7 times." Unlimited forgiveness. The #7 is a perfect number in Jewish tradition. The greatness of God's forgiveness shown to the woman taken in adultery.

2. Christ's example in humility

Humility is another necessary part of the Christian life. The book of Proverbs tells us that "Pride goeth before destruction and a haughty spirit before a fall." 16:18. Naaman's heart was lifted up in pride and he almost missed a blessing.

Nebuchadnezzar allowed his heart to become lifted up in pride. For that reason God drove him into the forest to eat grass like a beast for 7 long years.

Jesus said "Take my yoke upon you and learn of me. For I am meek and lowly in heart." Matt 11:29. An example of meekness was well demonstrated when Jesus, after supper, washed his disciples' feet. John 13:

Let this mind be in you, which was also in Christ Jesus. Phil 2:5

"Wherefore God hath highly exalted Him.

No title

Cold Spring Baptist Church — October 13, 1957 11:00 a.m.

On last Sunday I spoke on the subject, "How little is Little Rock." My reason for using such a subject was to break down any false idea anyone might have about prejudice, bigotry, segregation and integration as being confined to certain areas only.

I went on to point out that wherever one man was found with the idea he is superior to his fellowman. And progresses from superiority to supremacy, one human being more than another human being more than another human being(sic) you have a "Little Rock" that is not quite so little. I want to speak to you from this subject this morning.

"Where do we go from here" John 6: 68

This is a question of great importance in America today. It is a question of great concern around the civilized world. The whole world, at this sad hour in history is ablaze with race hatred, which has resulted into complete disregard for human rights, law and order in many places. God placed a high value on human life because he is the giver. And He reached into His bosom and gave His only begotten Son to save all mankind from degradation. But man, with his selfish heart and narrow mind, has lowered that high value of human life cheaper than the bullet it takes to destroy it.

So long as we disregard a neighbor as a neighbor. So long as we discredit the doctrine of the Fatherhood of God and the brotherhood of man. The value of human life will mean very little to us. Where do we go from here?

Let us turn to the Holy Bible for interpretation of the signs of the times. The Bible says: "In the last days perilous times shall come. For man shall be lovers of their ownselves, covetous, boasters, proud, lovers of pleasure more than lovers of God." That time is here.

The Bible also says: "The time will come when they will not endure sound doctrine." That time is here.

Again the Bible speaks: "And ye shall hear of wars and rumors of wars: For nation shall rise against nation, and Kingdom against Kingdom; and there shall be famines, and pestilences and earthquakes in divers places. All these are the beginning of sorrow. That time is also here.

Where do we go from here? Back to God!

Go back to where we left God and walk with him again. This is the time that men must return to God and live. Or turn from Him and die. Jesus said; "I, and I, If I be lifted up will draw all men." "And whosoever believeth in me shall never die." We must put Jesus back in our private lives. We must invite Jesus at the head of the conference table of world affairs.

All churches today would have an over flow of members if they could:

1. Join a church and have absolutely no responsibilities.

2. Pay a dollar a week and in return get a bonified contract on Heaven guaranteeing them admission with no questions asked by St. Peter.

Many more thousands would have gladly followed Christ. But they did not like His words.

1. "Love your neighbor"

2. "Do unto others"

3. "What does it profit a man"

4. "Except a man eat of my flesh and drink of my blood he hath no life in him"

"I am the bread of life."

These disciples did not like his words, so they went back. They took leave of Him. They forsook Him. So He returns to the twelve(12) "Will ye also go away?"

Remember Jesus had just fed these people (5000) on the Mt. side. Now they were full and had no further need of food. They began to regard Jesus with a suspicious eye. They said "How can we eat of this man's flesh and drink His blood?" This is a hard saying. So they went away. To the twelve, "Will ye also go away?" "Lord to whom shall we go?"

Divine Promises — 2nd Peter 3: 9

Cold Spring Baptist Church — October 27, 1957 11:00 a.m.

The Apostle Peter who wrote the letter from which our text is taken seems to have done very little writing. Having wrote only two Epistles, 1st Peter and 2nd Peter. He was not in a sense the original Peter, impulsive and full of weaknesses, whom Christ called "Simon". Christ often had to rebuke Simon Peter, in a gentle sort of way, because of his contentious spirit.

"Simon, Simon, behold Satan hath desired to have you that he may sift you as wheat. But I have prayed for thee that thy faith fail not" etc. Luke 22:31

The Gospel of Christ is able to change any man no matter how mean he may be. It might take a little (time) but it cannot fail. Because the "Gospel is the power of God unto salvation to all that believe." The Gospel changed Peter from a weakling to a "Rock". A great champion of the church who when the end of his career came, he was not afraid to give his life for the cause. The Gospel changed Saul the most sensational persecutor of the Church, Etc.

The central theme of Peter's letter was victory. Victory in Jesus Christ the greatest name given among men.

1. Victory over self. Many people have no self-control.

2. Victory over temptation.

3. Victory over suffering. Every child of God must suffer in some manner at some time.
a. We are the target of the infidel.
b. We are the target of lying tongues
c. We are the target of weak Christians

But Peter is very encouraging "For I am persuaded that the suffering of this present time." etc. Peter encouraged the Church to hold on and hold out. Just as the angry seas and fierce winds racked the little fishing boat as the disciples struggled to cross the stormy lake. So the world will rack the Church while it sojourns here.
a. Your faith will be sorely tried.
b. Your patience will be hard pressed.
c. Your reputation will be assassinated by your close friend.
But in all this remember the word of the text:
"The Lord is not slack, etc."

The Promises of God are contained in a nutshell in the Sermon on the Mount. All the promises of God to Israel. The true essence of all the Psalms of David were rehearsed by Jesus in that wonderful sermon on the mount.

1. Blessed are the poor in spirit
2. Blessed are they that mourn for
3. Blessed are the meek for they
4. Blessed are they which do hunger
5. Blessed are the merciful for
6. Blessed are the pure in heart
7. Blessed are the peacemakers . . .

Matt. 6:31 Take no thought for your life. What ye shall eat, or what ye shall drink. Nor yet for your body what ye shall put on. Is not the life more than meat. And the body than raiment. "But seek ye first the kingdom of God. etc."

Last, but not the least He has promised us a home. The other day before he left here He said "I go to prepare a place for you, etc." "In my Father's house." But in the meantime "Be thou faithful until death." Paul said "If this earthly house" Job said "I know that my Redeemer liveth."

Mortgage burning ceremony at Cold Springs Baptist Church – 1959

Dad with members of the Cold Springs' Trustee Board

Mortgage burning ceremony at Cold Springs Baptist Church – 1959
Dad at podium, Rev. Burney C. McCarley, Pastor of St. John's Baptist Church (immediate left)
and Rev. N.A. Mason, Pastor of New Hope Baptist Church (immediate right)

It is Later than You Think — Matt 24: 32, 33, 44

Cold Spring Baptist Church – March 23, 1958 11:00 am

The fig tree is one of the commonest trees of Palestine. And its budding is a sure sign of spring. "The trees of the field know their appointed time." Jesus used the fig tree as a striking contrast that the hatreds and wars among men, with famines, pestilences and earthquakes in divers places, are sure signs of His coming and the end of the world. He also said: "Many would come in my name saying I am Christ."

Jesus weeps over Jerusalem. We have only one other example of Jesus weeping. He may have wept many times more. Jesus had climbed one of the high hills over-looking the city. As he looked down he saw many different scenes; little children at play in the streets merchants bringing their long caravans into the city there were the ever-present soldiers looking for trouble beggars sat by the wayside

His thoughts were not filled with what he saw. But his thoughts were about mankind he came to save; "I came unto my own", etc. Now the "hour had come". The most crucial moments of his life were near at hand. In a few days he would be nailed to a wooden cross.

"O Jerusalem, Jerusalem, thou that killest the prophets and stowest them which are sent unto you, how often I would have gathered thy children together, even as a hen gathereth her chickens under her wings and you would not." Behold, your house is left unto you desolate. One of the Prophets had spoken of Jesus "As being despised and rejected of men. A man of sorrows acquainted with grief."

1. His disciples came to him and said "Master, see what manner of stores and what buildings are here?" There shall not be left one stone upon another." **It is later than you think.**

We are living in the "last days" Jesus spoke about. Paul, that dynamic young preacher who according to his own words was, "one born out of due season", said about the last days: "The time will come when men would not endure sound doctrine" but after their own lusts, etc.

It is later than you think
N.D.

Jesus said as it were in the days of Noah, so will it be in the coming of Christ, etc.

The world today, our world, is just as far away from God as in the days of Noah. We have taken our scientists for prophets. We have gone space crazy. God has become too slow for us. Someone said "God will answer prayer but some of us now consider God a failure. We don't need God anymore. Why we have super highways and sky ways; rocket ships, satellites and tranquilizing pills.

That same Jesus who wept over Jerusalem weeps today over the ignorance of men. According to God's time-table, **it's later than you think.**

Churches who conduct record hops to raise money**; It is later than you think.**

Hypocrites and false pretenders who hold the word of God in contempt**; It is later than you think.** Numbers players and drunks; **It is later than you think.**

Part-time Christians; **It's later than you think**.

But to the saved we have the assurance of God's word. Looking for and waiting unto the coming of the day of God, etc. 2 Peter 3

Making A Choice – John 6: 66-68

Cold Spring Baptist Church — June 8, 1958 11:00 am

Many, many people end up in life a bitter failure. All because they either make the wrong choice that climaxed in a sad state of disappointment, or they lived a whole life-time and were never quite able to make a decision. This is a right decision. Most of us read in our papers last week the story of a young man, only 21 years of age, sentenced to die in the electric chair. Although the jury, 12 people tried and true citizens of the community had recommended mercy for him. But mercy was denied.

All of this could have been avoided in the first place. But he made the <u>wrong</u> choice. Crime does not pay and prejudice does not pay.

Life is largely made up of choices – we choose vacations – we choose life partners for marriage – we choose between right and wrong course of action. But the choice by which to settle <u>all other</u> choices wisely is the choice of God. Whatever life's problems may be we should acknowledge God and His supreme wisdom as sufficient to all our needs. The Psalmist urged all Israel "In all thy ways acknowledge God"

Him and He will direct paths. One day Joshua challenged Israel, God's elect to make a choice.

1. They were now in that long cherished promised land

2. Had their place in the sun among other nations

3. Life for them soon became a luxury; lived in houses of hewn stone; slept on beds of ivory, listened to sweet music of the harp and viola; but step by step they withdrew; drifted from their God

4. Joshua now an old man saw danger; idolatry and sin creeping to strangle a new nation; he pleaded with them; "If it seems evil to you to serve the Lord; choose you this day whom ye will serve, etc . . . . but as for me and my house, etc . . . . we will serve the Lord." (Pro 1: 23 – because I have called and ye refused, etc.)

5. One day the 12 former fisherman of Galilee were required to make a choice

6. A great multitude had surrounded Jesus; Jesus knew their insincerity "Ye seek me because ye did eat of the loaves and were filled." Labor not for the meat that perishieth", etc.

Jesus knows our hearts. The crowd that followed Him was, no doubt, the same crowd who went out to see John the Baptist. In that crowd were sinners of the worst sort. In that crowd were speculators, hypocrites and criticizers. He had no words of praise or commendation for them. "O Ye generations of vipers who have warned you." Jesus said to them "I am the Bread of Life." "Your fathers did eat bread in the wilderness and are dead." "I am the living Bread." "Except ye eat my flesh – Drink of my Blood – Ye have no life." You are dead – <u>living, breathing</u> but spiritually dead.

Jesus went on to define the principals of the Kingdom and to expound the word of life. They begun to walk away; they walked away from <u>light to darkness</u>; they walked away from truth to error to Satan's lies. They walked away from <u>life</u> to <u>death</u>; they walked away from <u>Heaven</u> to <u>journey to hell</u>.

Jesus turned to the twelve. "Will ye also go away?" Peter spoke "To whom shall we go?" To heathen philosophers like Plato, Aristotle or Socrates and die? We have made our choice "Thou hast the words of eternal life."

God's Eternal Call to Man – Isa. 6: 6-8

N.D.

If you carefully noticed the reading of the text God needed someone. But He did not call anyone by name. He simply said: "Whom shall I send and who will go for us."

Now God used the pronoun "us". By that it is meant some other personality beside God was present. And God consulted him, "Who will go for us." Isaiah heard the voice of God and he responded, "here am I, send me."

Do you want to know why Isaiah replied so promptly? Here is why. Isaiah had a desire to work for God. He wanted to be useful in God's service. He wanted God to take him and use him; what a better world this would be if we had more men and women with a willing mind like Isaiah, who would be willing enough to shoulder their Christian responsibilities as they should and ought.

We live in this world but once and that life is all too short. Like the Psalmist said: "We spend our years as a tale that is told. We are soon cut off and we fly away. All men are called to a life of service. Jesus said "if any man will come after me let him; first deny himself; deny self of the pleasures and riches and luxuries of this world which are only deceiving, and take up the cross of Christ and follow him daily.

God is eternally seeking man. Ever since man violated the law of God and turned his back on him God has been seeking for man. God first looked for man in the usual place in the Garden. But he was not there. Adam was hiding behind excuses in a remote corner of the Garden. But God found him. God is seeking man today. He is calling him to a consecrated life.

God is asking man to surrender his life in full in order that He may use him to His glory and honor. Secondly, God is calling man to a life of service. "Go ye into my vineyard and work. And whatsoever is right I will pay you." God is calling man to a life of Holiness that man may no more sin but live a life without sin which is only possible in Jesus Christ. Man cannot live a good life by his own power. Jesus is calling all men to "Abide in me and I in you."

There are many men who reject God or fail to recognize the existence of the Divine, who count His way unholy. Now this is a bad situation that man will enjoy the blessings of Almighty God and all the benefits of nature. All these things come from God. They were brought about by the power of God. Yet they will discredit God for the very breath that they draw. They will discredit God even though in Him, according to the Scriptures, "we live, move and have our being." Now here is what God has to say: Because I have called and ye rescued etc. Prov. 1: 24-28.

- If Abraham had refused the call of God, he would never have become the father of the faithful.

- If Moses had refused to investigate the burning bush in the desert he would never have become a great instrument in leading Israel out of Egypt.

- If the child Samuel had ignored the small, still voice of God night after night while he slept in the Temple, he would not have become the first Prophet and judge of Israel.

- If Saul of Tarsus who was a potential enemy of the early church had refused the call of God on the Damascus road; had not gotten up from the dust and grit to answer "Lord, what would Thou have me do?" He would never have become the Apostle to the Gentiles; to have written 13 letters to all the churches of Asia Minor and Europe. And at the closing days of his life, as he waited for the executioner as his time was running out; called for his writing scroll and wrote to Timothy, his son in the Gospel, "I have fought . . . (end not found)

What God Can Do with One Man – 1 Samuel 12: 20, 23
Cold Spring Baptist Church – April 5, 1959 11:00 a.m.

Samuel prays for a sinful nation 7 ch.

Samuel lived a dedicated life – from infancy prayer was major in his life. His mother prayed for a man-child because she was barren. In those days, it was felt that for a woman to be barren was a curse from God. In our day it is just the opposite. There are some wives who feel it is a curse to have children. This is evidenced by the way some children are so shamefully neglected by some present day mothers.

Samuel had the distinction of being both Prophet, Priest and the last judge of Israel. He was called on to pray in a very dark house in the history of Israel.

His prayers saved the nation from being destroyed by her enemies.

What god can do with <u>one</u> dedicated man. With Abraham, God called forth a new nation. Abraham had the qualities of leadership God needed for a great task.

With Moses, God delivered an oppressed people.

With Martin Luther King of Montgomery, Ala., God has shown again He is a God of prayer.

Conclusion: what God can do with you if you will only give yourself whole-heartedly to Him? After all you cannot give to God material gifts to substitute your hearts.

Sin Is the Cause : The Hidden Wedge — Joshua 7: 20-22
Cold Spring Baptist Church — May 31, 1959 11:00 a.m.

Sin is an unpopular subject in our day. Yet sin is widespread. Everywhere you turn you see sin, sin and more sin. There was a time when preachers preached against the ugliness of sin and the awfulness of hell. Today, the Gospel is being preached without saving power. We hear today sermons without Christ. We try to save men without mentioning the Cross of Christ or the facts of His Resurrection. "For the preaching of the cross is foolishness to those that perish but to us." etc.

Whether we accept or ignore the facts, sin is a reality, and sin is universal. The Bible says: "All have sinned and come short of the Glory of God." "If we say we have not sinned we make Him a liar and His word is not in us." 1 John 1: 3, 10

Now, Sin is the cause of many hardships we have to suffer in our lives. "Whatsoever a man soweth that shall he also reap." Later in this message I want to talk about:

1. Sin sickness
2. Gossip and idle talks is sin
3. Men and women living together as husband and wife — unmarried — is sin
4. But right now I want to talk about sin in Israel. Re-read the text: Joshua 7: 10, 11

1. When Moses came to the end of his journey God had already prepared Joshua to take his place.

2. Moses death on Mt Nebo

3. Joshua in command

4. God's assurance to Joshua

5. Joshua succeeds at Jericho

6. But he fails at Ai

7. The concealed sin of Achan

A House Divided Cannot Stand : Let there be no divisions among you
Mark 3:25; Joshua 23:2; 24:14-15
Cold Spring Baptist Church — February 28, 1960 11:00 a.m.

The subject has a double meaning. It has its physical meaning and also its spiritual application. We know that in the physical sense a divided house will fall because it has no structural support. Also a house with a faulty foundation will fall. Jesus said in Mark 3:25 "And if a house be divided against itself, that house cannot stand." Jesus gave a parable of two builders. One builder wanted a house that would stand the test of time so he dug down deep in search of rock for a solid foundation. Jesus Christ is our foundation. The pillars of our spiritual house should be faith and truth.

The other builder simply wanted a house. When testing time came his house fell and great was the fall thereof. Cyanide, quickest, most deadly, most agonizing of poisons. Do you know the quickest way to kill a Church? By letting divisions come in the Church. A Church is made up of people. Also a social club or secret fraternity or baseball club is made up of people. But the difference between a Church and a social club is the Spirit of God.

And the Spirit of God will not dwell in an un-clean place. It will not dwell in a "house of confusion". The Church at Corinth was divided, split wide open. Some were following Paul, some Apollis and some Cephas. Paul heard the news and he pleaded with them, O Corinthians "Is Christ divided?" was I, Paul "crucified for you?" or "were you baptized in the name of Paul?" "I speak to your shame."

Christian friends, as members of the "Body of Christ" we must all stand together or we will all perish together. Together we stand but divided we fall. When Abraham

Lincoln was fighting the Civil War, he was fighting not so much to prove who was right, the north or the south. He was fighting not so much to set the Negro slaves free. But his aim and solemn purpose was to preserve the Union. Because a house divided cannot stand. We must come together or we will split asunder. Joshua spent a life-time trying to hold together the House of Israel. Joshua knew the importance of being together.

When Joshua was under Moses he saved the day by telling the truth. He was one of the 2 spies who brought back a faithful report. 10 others had caused a confusion in the camp. Before Moses died God told Moses to anoint Joshua to be his successor. When Joshua took command God assured him "As I was with Moses so will I be with you. Only be thou strong and of good courage." Joshua had great success because God was on his side.

Too Late — Luke 16:24-26
Cold Spring Baptist Church — April 1960

How the subject came about; the search for a text

Intro.: The man in business watches his sales volume closely and with concern. If the drop in sales is sharp, he jumps into action, before it is too late.

A mother watches over health of her children. She must be ready to protect before it is too late.

We have common words in our language we use every day that disturbs us somewhat such as, "A has been", "too old", "a cheat", " a liar", "a theif", "no good". But none of these words affect us like the words, "I am sorry you are too late."

Too late for that new job

Too late for the train

Too late for the deal

Our church needs to wake up before it's too late. We need to realize, as never before that together we stand but divided we fall. We need to realize, as never before, that you can have only one leader. Everybody can't lead at the same time. And nobody can lead for the Pastor. Nobody but the Pastor is responsible for the Church. Jesus called, ordained and commissioned Pastors only. Any person who is trying to take the Pastor's place need to find your own place and stay there before it is too late. We need God but God can get along without us. He got along quite well before we came on the scene.

Jesus said "A certain rich man" A rich man who waited too late to repent, etc. And a poor man named "Lazarus" Judas waited too late to repent. The rich farmer waited too late.

For Which of Those Works do ye Stone Me — John 10: 30-32
Cold Spring Baptist Church – May 15, 1960

1. In the text we can observe, to some degree, sadness, disappointment and pity had affected Jesus as the solicited from his opposers, the reason or reasons why they wanted to stone him. For He knew very well "They hated him without a cause."

2. Stoning was an ancient way of executing a wrong doer. It dates back to Israel while they were 40 years in the wilderness when the people no longer wanted to hear Moses, their leader. God told Moses He would come down on the Mount. But He charged Moses to charge the people not to touch even the foot of the Mount, man or beast or, they would be stoned to death.

Also in Leviticus the law states any man who blasphemes against God must be stone to death. We have an example of a man who, together with his whole family, was stoned to death for concealing his sins.

We have another example where the little thing we call conscience stopped the stoning of a woman taken in adultery.

If a man would only listen as his conscience trys to speak to him. He could avoid many embarrassing situations. We stone one another today with words of bitterness.

"For which of those works do ye stone me? Jesus' one and only purpose in coming to this world was to "Seek and save the lost. He sought neither fame nor glory from man.

1) Will ye stone me because I talked with Nicodemus one night?
2) Will ye stone me for restoring the sight of a man born blind?
3) Will ye stone me for healing the man who had an infirmity for 38 years?
4) Are you angry because I said "I and my Father are one?"
5) Or, just why will ye stone me?

The Preacher and His Task – II Timothy 4: 1-2

N.D.

1. The Preacher's call – Isaiah 6: 9 – Qualifications II Tim 3
2. The Preacher's Commission – Matt 28: 19-20
3. The Preacher's Responsibilities (the keys of the Kingdom) Paul (Acts 20: 28)

Why is the man of God so Important – because God speaks thru him to the people. Whenever God wanted to tell Israel anything He always called Moses. A Preacher is one who is called and chosen by God to proclaim his Gospel. The Preacher has the greatest job on earth. A unique position: he is a mediator. He pleads to God in behalf of man and he pleads to man on behalf of God. "Come and let us reason together." Isaiah said: "All day long, I have stretched forth my hands to a gainsaying and disobedient people."

Preaching is of paramount importance

The Preacher would not stand in his pulpit if he did not expect to touch and change individual loves. (Page 14 The Preacher). The main task of the Preacher is to Preach and teach the Gospel, baptize believers and minister to the sick. All other things are secondary to his calling. Once upon a time the minister was engaged in many things including waiting on tables. A murmuring went up among the Greeks. They felt they were being neglected. The question rose up in the early church of the minister's position had to be settled. So they called them together. "Look ye out" whom the Lord calls, the Lord also qualifies. Isaiah's readiness to proclaim God typifies the minister. The compelling hand of God was on the man.

The words of our text are part of the last letter and final benediction the Apostle Paul sent to young Timothy his son in the Gospel. At this time Paul was a prisoner at Rome waiting to be executed on the chopping block for the cause of Christ. His thoughts at this time were not so much about the axe that would server his head from his body. But his thoughts were about the word of God. Once he said "For me to live is Christ but to die is gain." He was not afraid to be absent from a frail body.

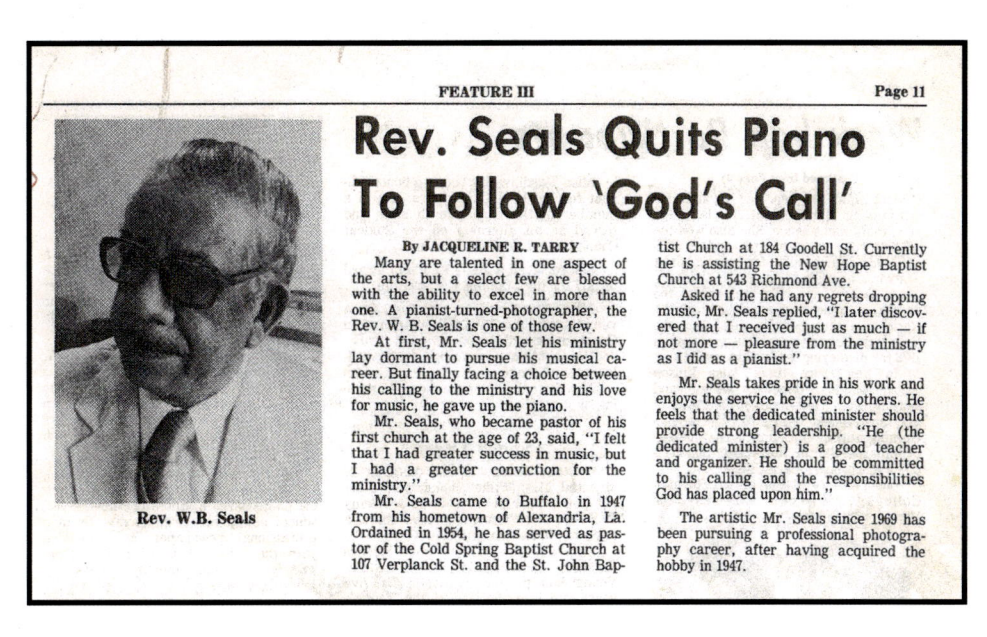

> **FEATURE III**   Page 11
>
> ## Rev. Seals Quits Piano To Follow 'God's Call'
>
> **By JACQUELINE R. TARRY**
>
> Many are talented in one aspect of the arts, but a select few are blessed with the ability to excel in more than one. A pianist-turned-photographer, the Rev. W. B. Seals is one of those few.
>
> At first, Mr. Seals let his ministry lay dormant to pursue his musical career. But finally facing a choice between his calling to the ministry and his love for music, he gave up the piano.
>
> Mr. Seals, who became pastor of his first church at the age of 23, said, "I felt that I had greater success in music, but I had a greater conviction for the ministry."
>
> Mr. Seals came to Buffalo in 1947 from his hometown of Alexandria, La. Ordained in 1954, he has served as pastor of the Cold Spring Baptist Church at 107 Verplanck St. and the St. John Baptist Church at 184 Goodell St. Currently he is assisting the New Hope Baptist Church at 543 Richmond Ave.
>
> Asked if he had any regrets dropping music, Mr. Seals replied, "I later discovered that I received just as much — if not more — pleasure from the ministry as I did as a pianist."
>
> Mr. Seals takes pride in his work and enjoys the service he gives to others. He feels that the dedicated minister should provide strong leadership. "He (the dedicated minister) is a good teacher and organizer. He should be committed to his calling and the responsibilities God has placed upon him."
>
> The artistic Mr. Seals since 1969 has been pursuing a professional photography career, after having acquired the hobby in 1947.
>
> *Rev. W.B. Seals*

Reprinted with permission from the Buffalo Challenger

This interview with Dad was printed in a special edition of the Buffalo Challenger or the Buffalo Criterion. This special insert has no date on newspaper banner. However, the interview provides a rare glimpse into my father's decisions about his career path. In this interview he describes his struggle of whether to follow his musical calling or his ministerial one.

Although the article says that he ultimately chose "God's Call", it also seems that he realized that the "Call" extended to a musical ministry. He made numerous contributions in many of the churches he served, from those in Louisiana to Buffalo. He directed and played for numerous choirs, founded the Bells of St. John's and gave piano lessons to many students; children and adults in our home, the student's homes or the church.

Jesus Said Unto Her, "I am the resurrection and the Life" John 11: 23-25

A Funeral — March 26, 1987

Members of the bereaved family; relatives of the deceased; and all our friends here today. It is always with sadness of heart and tear filled eyes when we come together here to say a sad good bye to one we loved so dear in life.

Our loved one, this member of the family, has gone on a long journey and our goodbyes are different from those we say at the train station, or airport. When we hug and kiss, wave with our hands and say "Have a nice trip."

This trip, this young man, our love one has taken is a one way trip. It will not bring the traveler back. As long as mankind is on this earth there will be trips and more trips. Nobody will be exempted and nobody will be overlooked.

Heb. 9: 27 tells us, "It is appointed unto man once to die, but after this the judgment." We call Death the King of Terror! We see Death as being cruel, very cruel. We see him as a destroyer, a thief in the night. We know death will snatch a little baby out of its mother's arms without apologizing. But we also know that Death can be a welcome relief from those, who could not get well, those who have suffered so much, for so long a time.

Please let me recommend to you today the One Man that is able to block the chariot wheels of death. The one and only man that can wipe away our tears today. And say to us "Let not your hearts be troubled. And if you have lost your way, we hear Him say, "I am the way, etc."

If you do not have a shelter over your head, again we hear Him, "In my Father's house are many mansions." If you are tired, we hear Him say, "Come unto me all ye that labor and are heavy laden and I will give you rest."

Family Reflections

Seals Family Reunion – 2005

By today's standards the Seals Family is a rather large one. Our parents had nine children, Willie Patterson, John Douglas, Mildred Irene (Wiggins), James Charles, Barbara Ann (Nevergold), Gerald, Kenneth, Bruce Ellis and David Alan. Dad died on April 19, 1995 and our mother, Clara Ellis Seals died on December 24, 2005.

One son, Dr. Kenneth, MD pre-deceased our mother. He died on May 25, 1996.

Our parents had 19 grandchildren at the time of their deaths. They also have 28 great grandchildren and 7 great—great—grandchildren and of course the family continues to grow. The photo above pictures members of the Seals Clan at the family's reunion in Buffalo. Family members now live in Georgia, California, Colorado, Tennessee, North Carolina, Virginia, Washington, D.C. and other parts of New York State.

A number of his children have written short articles of their remembrances of our father's activities as a minister. I should note here that the age differences between us span over 30 years from the oldest, Willie to the youngest, David. So, the reflections provide some insight into the development of our father's ministerial avocation, as each of us experienced it.

Remembrance of Dad as a Minister – David Alan Seals

Being the youngest of dad's children, I was not born during his most active time in the ministry. While Dad was an associate pastor at St. John's Baptist Church in Buffalo, he did not preach very often. But my most vivid memory of him in the pulpit was when he was the interim pastor at New Hope Baptist Church in Niagara Falls, New York. I was probably around 13 or 14 years old at the time.

We'd get up a little earlier than normal to take the ride to Niagara Falls, which was about a 20 to 30 minute trip as I recall. The drive would take us through Grand Island New York, traveling over two big bridges to get to Niagara Falls.

Once we arrived, the parishioners were very open to us and very respectful of Dad. This was the second time Dad was interim pastor. More than any one particular sermon, I remember most Dads' physical presence in the pulpit. It was different than my normal view of him at home. He seemed very comfortable and very at ease with being in the public eye and speaking to the congregation. Looking back on it now, it's amazing that he had that poise, considering his formal education ended in the sixth grade.

Once in a while after church, we'd go to a member's home or out to a restaurant for dinner. It gave us more time to get to know the people and the church. At one point, I thought he was going to end up becoming the full time minister. But I think his love and history with St. John's and reluctance to leave Buffalo, prevented that move.

The other memory I have of Dad was the last time he preached at St. John's Baptist Church. I was in my early 20's. All of my brothers and sisters who were still in Buffalo surprised him by attending. He was extremely surprised to see us there. Dad's association with St. John's went back to the 1940s. I was always struck by the respect Dad received from church members.

Remembering our father — Mildred Seals Wiggins

In one of my father's Bibles, he has highlighted many passages of scripture. As I leaf through it many images remind me of him sitting at his small desk in the corner of the living room. It is there where he read, searched scripture and wrote his sermons. Page after page contain notes and references to coordinating events, subjects and parallels of God's desires for us. Our father's desire for us (his children) was to receive, remember and practice God's word in our lives always. Psalm 100, A Psalm of praise and encouragement for us all, was one of his favorite scriptures.

Reflections of Dad — Jerry Seals

I remember Dad preparing for his Sunday sermons, as a carefully crafted procedure that began early in the week. Sometimes on Tuesday or Wednesday evening, after dinner, he would sit at his desk, turn on the desk lamp, and open his Bible. He might have had a subject in mind even before he began to thumb through the pages: something relating to an incident which may have happened personally, or reported in the daily news, locally or nationally. In the Bible would be the parallel and the guidance that he could share with fellow parishioners. One of the things that always stood out for me was his thirst for knowledge. In his youth, schooling was not a priority for little black boys in the south.

He never went past the sixth grade of formal education but set about, with a strong curiosity, to educate himself. He once told me that when he was a boy that the house they lived in was so drafty that his mother used to stuff newspaper in the cracks of the walls to keep the wind out. He told me that by trying to pronounce the words in the paper, he taught himself to read. Preparing for a sermon, with a six grade formal education presented some problems though. Properly pronouncing some of the names and locations was often difficult, but he never hesitated or exhibited any concern for appearances when he asked my sister, who was in college, how to pronounce certain words. The lifelong quest for self-improvement superseded any false notion of parental superiority.

I remember, because the bedroom that I shared with my younger brothers was directly across from my parents, that he often read his Bible in bed, only because he read it out loud in what I think he thought was a whisper but that I can confirm was not. I know with a certainty that his utmost concern was to get it right. To deliver the message as he intended so that every listener could understand, consider and perhaps apply it in their own lives

There is nothing new in the world. Everything that is has already been. The history of Being is the Bible, God's law, the sacrifice of Jesus, the redemption of man. He died for our sins that we might have everlasting life.

My father wasn't perfect, but what human being is? The funny thing about his imperfections is that I don't really think anyone would consider them a big deal. But he did! On Friday night we had fish for dinner. I really looked forward to Friday. Fish and French Fries! Fresh Haddock! My mother was the best cook ever and she prepared meals with the greatest love and dedication, seven days a week. On Friday they liked to have a glass of beer with their fish. It was the only day that I remember them ever doing it but my father would not if he had to go to church, counsel a church member, or visit the sick and shut in, which he did increasingly as his career began to wind down. I feel that he thought it was improper for a minister to perform his duties with even a hint of beer on his breath. I used to laugh about it then. I think I more understand his point now. He was attempting, not only to advise, speak, and reveal the gospel, but to be a living example. If the parishioner, in search of comfort and relief from the pressures of life, have an example, free of corruption, they have that rock on which they can endure whatever pressures they might be feeling in their daily lives.

Dad was a rock for us as well. Every morning at 5:30 am he got up, for 25 years, got bathed, dressed, ate his breakfast, and went to work at the Chevrolet motor plant. He was hardly ever sick, hardly ever late, and never missing in action. In a time when many black families were often without a father figure, he was steadfast. He was our bread winner. He was our hero! Our male authority. One of the worst things my mother could say to me was, "I'm going to tell your father when he gets home!" It was then that I knew that I was in trouble. And the mischief that I'd gotten myself into was going to be resolved in a way that I would not find especially pleasant. It wasn't that I was a bad kid but somehow I always wound up doing what I shouldn't be doing. I now appreciate what I didn't at the time and have tried to incorporate that same level of responsibility, respect, and love that I benefited from into raising my children.

Besides his career in ministry, I would be remiss if I didn't speak to his many other attributes. His musical ability is well known. As a pianist, he was a performer, music teacher, and founder of the Bells of Saint John's gospel choir. I grew up listening to him play the piano in our living room, Beethoven, Rachmaninov and others. I was also surprised to learn that earlier in his life he played in a small jazz band.

His photography business spanned more than forty years and Seals Ebony Studio was the choice for many of the residents of Buffalo's inner city who found his prices and quality photos their number one choice for family weddings, graduations, children's parties and many other occasions. What was most impressive to me, now, was his ability to compartmentalize all of his various interests and maintain a high level of accomplishment in all of the very different interests that he held. He read magazines, researched, experimented with techniques, and practiced them over and over again until he was satisfied with the result. I've seen him build a laundry room on the back of the house, from the ground up including framing, walling in, electrical, plumbing, and heating. He performed all of the expensive necessary repairs around the house to save the cost of having some outside company do it. He provided for and raised his family and more importantly lead by example.

Born in 1910, in Alexandria, Louisiana, a Black boy of mixed heritage had no chance, opportunity, prospects, or future. My dad proved that common theory false. He demonstrated that genius does not just reside in the affluent, the chosen, or the dominant culture. Not having opportunity he crafted it. Not having wealth he discovered it in family. Not being completely accepted as an interracial child, he stood tall and accepted himself. He found his ultimate calling as a minister of the gospel because I don't think he wanted any human being to feel the pain and rejection that he sometimes felt from both Blacks and Whites. His Father was White, his mother Black, his life was filled with contradiction. Yet his life was more filled with triumph and overcoming. My father will always have a profound effect on the person that I am and the person I am striving to be.

Remembrances of Dad — Willie Patterson Seals

Dad worked at D'Angelo's Fish Market in Alexandria in the 1930s. One day I was with Dad when he got paid. The money was counted out, one, two, three, four, five, six dollars for a week's work. To me it seemed like a lot of money and it had to feed two adults and four kids.

In Buffalo Dad's first car was an old Chevy with standard shift. He taught me to drive it but coordinating clutch, gas and gear shift was a horror. On one teaching session at Fillmore and Clinton, I was stopped by the red light and being on a slight hill I stalled the engine. I had trouble getting the clutch, gas and gears working properly and the car kept stalling. The cars behind blew their horns but I couldn't get the car moving. Dad got excited and yelled, "I swanney", "I swanney" and after a while I got the car moving. Dad never cursed but at times he would say "I swanney". Perhaps someone can tell me what that means.

Later I bought a 1950 Olds and when to Toronto but forgot to tell anyone. Driving back at 4 am I saw Dad peeking out the window looking for me. Seeing him made me feel terrible because he had been up all night and had to go to work at the Chevy plant in a couple hours. It also showed me how much he cared.

The last year of Dad's life was at the Deaconess Nursing Home. At that time I would visit him every Sunday after church and we would walk up and down the aisles and talk. I would say "Today is Sunday, it's beautiful, there's snow and cold"; "The church service was nice and there was a lot of singing". Then he'd say, "Did you preach?"-"Did you preach?" Then I'd say, "I can't preach." He looked down at the floor and shook his head and probably thought: You poor thing – you can't preach!

Barbara and parents, Rev. W. B. and Mrs. Clara Seals

Barbara accompanied her parents to the program honoring her father on the occasion of the Bells of St. John's 40th anniversary, 1988

Memories of Dad – Barbara Seals Nevergold

The sermons in this book represent over half of the sermons/sermon notes that Dad kept in the file cabinet in his attic office/photography studio. He also had thousands of negatives, which spanned the nearly 50 years of his photography business, in the same cabinet. It has always been my intention to preserve these precious documents and share them with the family, especially our youngest members. After finding these papers, I placed them in a manila folder and over the next few months I typed each one and saved on a hard disk.

However, I found the negatives and the photos they yielded more compelling. As a result, I immediately focused my energies on getting several exhibits produced and magazine articles written about Dad's photography business.

49

To complicate matters, in the years between typing up the sermon notes and the present time there have been major changes in the technology. When I returned to this project I found that I could not open up the old hard disks where the files were stored. I started over for this book and re-typed each one in a word document that is easily accessible. The sermons are presented in chronological order, from the earliest ones that we found through the early 1960s. There is also a funeral sermon from 1987. There are other examples from the 1980s, which are not in this edition but may be shared in a future publication.

Although these are hand-written notes with scratch outs and corrections, they illustrate the meticulous nature of Dad's sermon development. As my siblings have noted, he worked at his desk in the living room, where he wrote and practiced his sermons. I remember him asking me for the definition of a word or asking for my re-action to a particular thought or point he was trying to make. But I had no idea until I saw his notes how much work he put into writing his sermons and preparing to deliver them. It's obvious that he not only worked to anchor his sermons in the Word, but he also tried to make them relevant by relating the text to current events and everyday life. One amusing revelation that I've learned about my father from reading all of these notes is that he had a habit of using any paper at hand to write these sermons. He wrote on the back of letters and flyers, on small note cards and scraps of paper, and on lined and un-lined paper. I'm not sure if he was an early "green" enthusiast or just very frugal.

I think that the time and effort that Dad put into writing his sermons is also indicative of his work ethic and the way that he approached his employment and his other avocations; photography and music. He once told my husband Paul that when he worked in an auto parts store in Alexandria, he memorized the ID numbers and locations of every part in the store! He was a life-long learner and a self-taught learner. As a young man, he studied piano and became an accomplished pianist and organist of gospel and classical music.

After moving to Buffalo, he took up photography and quickly became a sought-after practitioner in that field. When I think of Dad, I see a man who was multi-talented and dedicated to self-improvement. I think he had great aspirations, but given the era and a large family to support and raise, his aspirations took a back seat to his every-day job at the Tonawanda Chevy Plant.

As for my memories of his ministerial work, I recall that Dad was a rather "academic" preacher. As I read his notes, it's clear that his sermons were researched and organized. And when he delivered his sermons, they were more like lectures. He didn't use most of the conventions that his peers used to elicit emotional responses from their audiences, e.g. call and response, the vocal, sing-song preaching style or the interjection of what could best be described as a grunt or "uh" to punctuate a sentence.

Many ministers use music to enhance their presentations and elicit congregational involvement, but Dad couldn't sing so he lacked the ability to incorporate song into his sermons. But his style did not adversely affect his ministry. He was often invited to be the guest speaker at many churches during his career. In addition, he served as the interim-pastor for lengthy periods at New Hope Baptist Church in Niagara Falls, New York, on two different occasions. From time to time, I still meet people from the church who express great respect and admiration for our father. I've also found numerous newspaper articles that announce Dad's visit to various churches as the guest minister for morning worship or special services.

Although he pastored several churches in Alexandria, I only know of one that he pastored in Buffalo; the Cold Spring Baptist Church. I was a teen ager during that time and I don't remember a lot of detail about that period. He built the church from a small congregation based in a house to a thriving membership headed to building a new church home. However, dissension in the church led to his leaving Cold Spring and returning to St. John. Some of the sermons in this volume allude to the problems at the church and are an indication of his attempt to end the discord.

A fond memory that I have of Dad's ministerial career has nothing to do with his preaching or pastoring; well, on second thought it is related to his preaching. There was a time when guest ministers, even if they were preaching at their own churches, were given a special donation or "love offering" for their services. The plate was passed and the congregation contributed to this separate offering for the guest minister. On those Sundays, when Dad would come home after church he'd empty the "love offering" bag (sometimes a brown paper one) of change and paper money. He'd then give me and my brothers the opportunity to take the pennies, nickels, dimes or quarters for ourselves. He was very generous in that way. I loved those Sundays!

Both our parents were very religious and required us to go to church and not just on Sunday morning. There was Sunday School, Sunday services and the Baptist Youth Training Union meetings, for example. Sundays were also movie day for the neighborhood kids at the old Lyceum Theatre on Broadway, around the corner from our apartment. But, the rule was, if you didn't go to church you didn't do anything else that day! Even after we got older and most of us stopped going to church regularly, my mother would tell us, "Just go to church, anybody's church!" I know she always prayed for us. Dad probably did too, but he was not as insistent about church attendance as Mom.

Dad continued to serve the Lord and the church well into his late 70s. He was appointed to St. John's visitation ministry and diligently visited the sick, whether they were in the hospital, nursing home or in their own residences until age curtailed his activities. Alzheimer's disease robbed him of the keen mind he used to excel in all his avocations; Minister of the Gospel, musician and photographer. But his decision to maintain his papers and photographic collection has provided tangible examples of the man and his contributions to his family and community. Finally, I would add the title of "community historian" to my father's resume. He preserved written and pictorial artifacts of an era and a community that document African Americans' contributions and accomplishments. As such, his sermons and photographs are an invaluable historical archive.

Made in the USA
Columbia, SC
27 April 2022